D1511618

WARBIRDS

WARBIRDS

Jeremy Flack

This edition published in 1996 by the
Promotional Reprint Company Ltd,
Kiln House,
210 New Kings Road,
London SW6 4NZ for
Booksales in New York, Chapters in Canada and Chris Beckett Ltd in New Zealand

ISBN 1 85648 331 2

Printed and bound in China

COVER: Republic P-47 Thunderbolt.
OPPOSITE: Spitfire HF Mk IXb MH434 flies with Kittyhawk Ia AK933 which is painted in the colours of No 112 Squadron, RAF when based in the Middle East.

CONTENTS

COMMUNICATIONS:

TRANSPORT:

TRAINERS:

INDEX

INTRODUCTION

Warbirds illustrates a representative cross-section of the surviving types of aircraft from World War 2 which are still flying. It is a companion book to *Spitfire* and *Fighters* which together give an overview of the current developments in the restoration and airshow world, providing a fascinating insight into the preserved and restored aircraft which grace our skies.

It is sad to say that these aircraft are only a small proportion of the total. Large numbers of World War 2 aircraft types appear to be extinct even as far as static exhibition is concerned. This makes restoration and replication crucial - but it is expensive. While many museums do not have sufficient resources to fund this sort of work, it is good to see that there are a number of individuals and organisations throughout the world that are trying to make a significant effort to reverse the situation. But unfortunately it does mean that, while the Supermarine Spitfires and North American P-51 Mustangs abound - indeed the number of airworthy examples seems to increase year by year - unusual types remain rare.

When an unusual aircraft is restored it creates much interest - for example, in the UK the Duxford-based Aircraft Restoration Company was responsible for the fine restoration of the only flyable Bristol Blenheim. The euphoria was dashed just one month after its first flight when the aircraft was lost in a flying accident. Such was the restoration team's determination and resolve to see a flying Blenheim that they turned around and started another project. Their motivation and dedication has seen the restoration of a second Blenheim - and what a superb job it is. (Photos of both Blenheims can be seen in this book, pp40-41.) Over the Atlantic, in the USA, another project will soon result in the completion of major restoration work - airworthy Messerschmitt Me262 jets. Here, an original Me262 was placed with Classic Fighter Industries and the Texas Airplane Factory for restoration as a static exhibit for Naval Air Station Willow Grove. During the job each of the parts was used as a pattern and reverse engineered. The result is that in addition to a fully restored static aircraft for the museum, four 'new' Me262s will soon be seen in the air - and appreciated by hundreds of thousands more people than the static example.

This highlights one of the dilemmas of museums. Take the huge US Smithsonian Collection: like other museums it has a reserve collection of aircraft - but only some of these can be seen at Silver Hill and many are stored and unlikely to see light of day. They aren't always completely safe in storage: more than one aircraft has been lost to fire while stored. It is to be hoped that the example of the Me262s may lead to similarly beneficial arrangements.

Only a few years ago an airworthy Messerschmitt Bf109 was unthinkable and yet today there are two based at Duxford. In Canada a restoration project is coming to its conclusion which will increase the number of airworthy Mitsubishi A6M Zeros by half. While the Spitfire has seen a great deal of restoration activity over the last decade or two, the number of airworthy Hurricanes has doubled and with the number of restoration projects currently in progress, this will continue.

It is good to see that major companies are getting involved in restoration projects. As an example Lufthansa has set up its Heritage Flight which has seen the Ju52/3m operation established to tour around Europe and operate flights for those that are interested in travelling at a more leisurely pace or merely sampling flights of yesteryear. Similar civil projects have already been achieved by other smaller organisations with aircraft such as the Douglas DC-3/C-47, the de Havilland Rapide and Ford Trimotor; their efforts can provide enjoyment to many while being economically self-sustaining.

While outside the scope of this book, the consideration of the Swiss Air Force to donate their retired Hawker Hunter fighters to suitable museums and collections is a welcome gesture. One can only hope that this will be repeated more by other air forces to enable some of the 1950s and 1960s era aircraft - the exciting postwar period which saw the transition from prop to jet - to be preserved for future generations.

One wonders how many aircraft types that have long been considered extinct might still be discovered. Attempts to recover aircraft from the icy wastes of Greenland or the hot and humid remote Pacific Islands have been undertaken for a number of years as they have from the lakes of Norway and Scotland. North Africa saw many major air battles and it seems likely that there are aircraft buried out there in the Sahara Desert under sand. In the meantime the pulling back of the Iron Curtain has already resulted in the recovery of a number of aircraft, some of which have already commenced restoration. While rumours will always abound of secretly hidden aircraft in obscure places occasionally they can prove to be true - like the Iraqi Sea Furies - and can make the lengthy task of research, detective work and hunting all the more worthwhile.

The abilities displayed by many of the restoration teams and companies to rebuild these aircraft to their original - if not better - condition is to be applauded. Long may they continue! Many of the restoration groups rely on a great deal of volunteer help to keep them going. Anybody who has some appropriate skills to offer or is interested in seeing or photographing these aircraft for themslves may find the list of contacts at the end of *Fighters* and *Spitfire* helpful.

Finally, I'd like to thank all the pilots and owners that have helped me to get into a position to take the photos in these books often to their inconvenience. A large thank-you as well goes to my wife Julie for vital support and encouragement.

FIGHTERS
AMERICAN

ABOVE: The Lockheed P-38 Lightning was a long-range fighter-bomber, nightfighter and the most widely used photo-reconnaissance aircraft of World War 2. Most were withdrawn at the end of the war although a few remained in service until 1949. Sadly only a few of the 9,923 P-38s built continue flying today.

LEFT: The Curtiss P-40 Warhawk was a useful fighter rather than outstanding. It was built in substantial numbers (13,783) mainly because it was available at the start of the war, exactly when it was needed. It was flown by the RAF as the Kittyhawk and Tomahawk and many remain flying today.

OPPOSITE: The Republic P-47 Thunderbolt was a long-range fighter whose role was to escort and protect large formations of bombers from marauding Luftwaffe fighters. 15,863 were built for the USAAF and RAF but only a few remain airworthy.

TOP: The Bell P-63 Kingcobra was an unusual fighter, with a large cannon firing through the propeller spinner and the engine located behind the pilot. Although 3,303 were built, it did not find favour with the USAAF and most served the Russians in the ground-attack role. Today it is a fairly rare beast.

ABOVE: The North American P-51 Mustang was the most popular of USAAF fighters and remains so today. Originally constructed for an RAF requirement, a total of 15,367 was built and large numbers still remain flying with individuals or flying collections.

OPPOSITE TOP: The Grumman F4F Wildcat fighter flew throughout the war although superseded by later more powerful types. Of the 7,815 built, a substantial number flew with the Royal Navy's Fleet Air Arm as the Martlet. Only a few remain airworthy and these were all built by GM as the FM-2.

OPPOSITE BOTTOM: The Vought F4U Corsair was powered by the P&W R-2800 Double Wasp, then the most powerful engine available. Recognisable by its distinctive inverted gull wing, some 12,000 were built and served with a number of countries. Like many fighters it was also capable of ground attack. It remains a much sought after warbird.

ABOVE: The Grumman F8F Bearcat was the US Navy's ulti-mate piston fighter. The small, light fuselage with a powerful engine gave tremendous performance. Large orders were placed but cut at the end of World War 2. Although on board carriers bound for the Pacific they arrived too late to see action. 1,266 were eventually built and are in great demand for air racing.

OPPOSITE TOP: The Grumman F7F Tigercat was intended to be a naval high performance fighter with unrivalled firepower.
Ordered in 1941, deliveries were so protracted that World War 2 finished before it was operationally deployed. Only 361 were built and the few that remain airworthy survived through their protracted use as fire bombers.

OPPOSITE BOTTOM: The Grumman F6F Hellcat was basically an advanced F4F Wildcat with a more powerful engine. It fought the Zero with devastating results and of the 12,275 built, 1,182 were delivered to the FAA. Relatively few now remain airworthy.

TOP: The Gloster Gladiator entered service during February 1937 and was used mainly in the Middle East during the early war years. Gladiators claimed some 250 kills and served with distinction in the protection of Malta. This Gladiator is in No 247 Squadron markings and is operated by the Shuttleworth Collection.

ABOVE: The Hawker Hurricane first flew in 1937 and served in greater numbers with the RAF during the early war years than any other fighter. Eventually, a total of 14,533 Hurricanes was built. The Santa Monica Museum of Flight owns this one.

BRITISH

TOP: The Hawker Sea Fury first flew in 1945 and became the Royal Navy's fastest piston-powered aircraft and its principal fighter until replaced by jets in 1953. This USA-based Sea Fury FB11 is owned by Ellsworth Getchell and is flown in Royal Australian Navy markings.

ABOVE: The Supermarine Spitfire first flew in 1936 and became the RAF's most prolific fighter of the war with 20,351 built. A firm favourite of pilots then and now, its design was such that, through continual development, it remained a front line fighter through to the early 1950s. This OFMC Spitfire IX is painted in the markings of No 222 Squadron.

GERMAN

ABOVE: The Bf109 was developed in secret for the emerging Luftwaffe in 1934 and flown the following year. A number saw operational service in Spain with the Condor Legion which flew in support of Franco's Nationalist forces. Using this experience, the Bf109 pilots were well trained for the outbreak of war and helped the Nazis overrun Europe. It wasn't until matched against Spitfires and Hurricanes that these fighters met their match.

The Bf109 development ran in parallel with the Spitfire in which one type would leapfrog in front of the other as new developments emerged. Because of these improvements, it remained in front-line use throughout the war; over 33,000 were built. Although German aircraft production collapsed towards the end of the war, further Bf109s were built in Czechoslovakia by Avia as the S-199 and CASA of Spain built the HA1112 (illustrated) which was powered by the Rolls-Royce Merlin. The HA1112s remained in use with the Spanish Air Force until 1967 and as a result a number remain. With only a couple of genuine Bf109s airworthy, a number of the HA1112s have had the Merlin replaced by the original Daimler-Benz to give the authentic look.

At the time of writing, no other World War 2 Luftwaffe fighters are flying although there are several projects currently aimed at changing this. Examples of the Fw190 are being restored and replica Me262s are likely to be flying shortly.

JAPANESE

ABOVE: The Mitsubishi A6M Zero was designed in 1937 to a precise Japanese Navy specification that only Mitsubishi was willing to attempt. The A6M1 first flew on 1 April 1939 but it was the more powerful A6M2 variant that first saw action in China. Here it completely outclassed all the opposition although its existence was ignored by top officials until the devastating attack on Pearl Harbor.

The Zero was capable of out-turning and out-climbing Allied fighters during the early period of the Pacific war and as such the Zero appeared to be a difficult adversary. However, during the Battle of Midway a Zero was captured virtually intact. Shipped to the USA, it was flown to gain as much data as possible. Effective tactics were devised and the design of the F6F tuned to take advantage of its weaknesses.

Although well in excess of 10,000 Zeros were built, due to the Allies' instruction that the Japanese war machine had to be destroyed the surviving Zeros were all but eliminated. Currently, only two US-based examples are airworthy.

ATTACK/BOMBERS

AMERICAN

OPPOSITE TOP, ABOVE AND LEFT: The Douglas A-26 Invader was designed as an attack bomber and nightfighter replacing the A-20 Havoc and first flew in 1942. Not flown operationally until 1944, the A-26 flew some 11,000 sorties over Europe dropping 18,000 tons of bombs for just 67 aircraft lost. A number of the 2,446 A-26s built continued to serve in Korea and Vietnam.

OPPOSITE BOTTOM: The Douglas AD-1 Skyraider was designed towards the end of the war to replace the SBD Dauntless and TBD Destroyer. However, deliveries to the USN did not commence until just after the war. Later redesignated A-1, the Skyraider saw extensive use in Korea and Vietnam.

TOP: The B-17, which became the USAAF's most famous bomber, bore the brunt of the offensive against Germany and occupied Europe. They suffered badly during the daylight raids until the arrival of long-range fighters. A total of 12,731 was built by Boeing, Douglas and Lockheed Vega. B-17G *Sally B* flies as a UK memorial to members of the USAAF 8th AF who lost their lives. Painted to represent various units, she displays here markings of the 457th Bomb Group.

LEFT: Escorted by P-51 Mustangs and a P-47 Thunderbolt, camouflaged *Sally B* sports the markings of 351st Bomb Group.

OPPOSITE TOP: *Sally B* in 709th Bomb Squadron, 447th Bomb Group markings.

OPPOSITE BOTTOM: Bristling with guns, the B-17G was intended to defend itself. It was fitted with 13 .50in guns in the nose, tail and turrets on top and below as well as in the dorsal position shown here.

TOP: Lone Star Museum's B-17G commences her journey from the UK to her new home at Houston in 1987 in the markings of *Thunder Bird* which flew 116 missions for the 303rd Bomb Group.

ABOVE: Nose gun positions together with mission markings and *Sentimental Journey* nose art on the CAF B-17.

OPPOSITE: *Sally B* painted in 324th Bomb Squadron, 91st Bomb Group colours for the film *Memphis Belle* and with her bomb doors open.

TOP AND OPPOSITE BOTTOM: The Consolidated B-24 Liberator was a long-range, high-speed bomber for the USAAF. A total of 19,256 was completed compared with just 12,731 B-17s or 7,377 RAF Lancasters. CAF-operated *Diamond Lil* is one of only a few B-24s still flying.

ABOVE: The North American B-25 Mitchell was designed as a light, fast, attack bomber and first flown in January 1939. Nearly 900 examples of this bomber were ordered for the RAF. The Duxford-based TFC B-25D Mitchell is painted with RAF D-Day markings and coded VO-B of No 98 Squadron.

OPPOSITE TOP: The EAA B-17G takes-off from Midland Airport through the smoke of a Confederate Air Force display.

ABOVE: Other operators of the B-25 were the US Navy and Marine Corps. This solid-nosed PBJ-1J is painted in the markings of the USMC and is fitted with four guns in the nose plus four mounted in fuselage blisters. Perhaps the most daring and famous raid undertaken by B-25 Mitchell aircrew was that led by Lt-Col Jimmy Doolittle. On 18 April 1942 16 B-25s took-off from the deck of the aircraft carrier USS *Hornet*. These aircraft hit a number of Japanese cities including Tokyo and, although the raid was not of strategic importance, it dealt a powerful psychological blow against the Japanese who thought that their mainland was beyond range of enemy aircraft. When President Roosevelt revealed that the raid had taken place from the secret base of 'Shangri-La', it also produced a psychological boost to the American public who were still suffering the indignation of Pearl Harbor.

The B-25B and B-25C saw improved armament, ordnance capacity and engine power, while the B-25G was fitted with a 75mm M4 cannon for attacking Japanese shipping. The B-25H was the most heavily armed variant with a 75mm cannon and four .50in guns in the nose plus a pair in blisters on either side of the nose. In addition, a twin-gun dorsal turret was fitted plus a waist gun on either side and a twin gun in the tail. It was also capable of carrying a 3,000lb bomb load. The US Navy and Marine Corps took delivery of Mitchells from January 1943 as the PBJ-1C followed by D, G, H and J models; in all a total of some 700 aircraft were delivered.

Some 11,000 B-25s were built and besides those flown by the USAAF, USN, Marines and RAF, they were also used by the air forces of Australia, Canada, Netherlands, Russia and the Free French as well as a number of additional postwar air forces.

OPPOSITE TOP AND BOTTOM: One side of TFC's B-25 has nose art which features the collection's logo, while the other has Walt Disney's cartoon character Grumpy painted on it.

ABOVE: This Mitchell was converted to a TB-25N trainer in military service before being modified into an chemical bomber. It has had this modification reversed and is now operated by the Confederate Air Force as *Yellow Rose*. Mitchells could be armed with up to 14 .50in machine-guns and a pair of these can be seen mounted in fuselage blisters plus another in the nose.

OPPOSITE TOP: The Dutch-based Duke of Brabant's Air Force B-25 Mitchell makes some smoke while it taxies out after a display at Duxford. The B-25J saw the reintroduction of the glazed nose for the bomb aimer although some later examples were fitted with solid noses. During 1943-44 a number of B-25 variants were converted to training aircraft in the AT-25 series and later redesignated as TB-25s. Postwar even more were converted of which the TB-25J was the most numerous with over 600 modified. During the early 1950s further con-

versions were carried out as flying classrooms for fire control radar instruction and multi-engined training.

OPPOSITE BOTTOM: The Confederate Air Force Boeing B-29 Superfortress starts up one of its four 2,200hp Pratt & Whitney R-3350 engines at Midland Airport prior to a pre-air-show air test. The Superfortress was conceived from the idea of an extremely long range, high altitude and large capacity bomber back in 1937. It wasn't until 1940 that the design gelled and on 21 September 1942 the prototype B-29 took to the air. Such was the confidence and need for this aircraft that orders totalling 1,664 B-29s had already been placed. The B-29 had an amazing 3,700-mile range with 20,000lb of bombs. It was the first military aircraft to provide a pressurised compartment for the whole crew. The first recorded operational use of the B-29 was on 5 June 1944.

ABOVE: *Fifi* - the only B-29 still flying - is owned by the Confederate Air Force. It was located on a USN range in the desert at China Lake, California along with a number of other B-29s awaiting use as targets. As the USAF had disposed of all of its B-29s the US Navy allowed the CAF to select one of them. A CAF team managed to get her flying again in just nine weeks and on 2 August 1971 she was flown to the then CAF HQ at Harlingen.

The B-29 was used exclusively in the Pacific theatre of operations. Initially hitting Japanese targets in China and Burma, progressing to mainland Japan as the Mariana Islands of Saipan, Guam and Tinian were recaptured, finally large formations of up to 500 B-29s commenced bombing Japan.

The high altitude bombing of industrial sites proved less effective than the lower level incendiary raids against easily combustible civilian houses. On 9 March 334 B-29s fire-bombed Tokyo. In the resulting inferno nearly 16sq miles of the city were destroyed and over 80,000 Japanese people died. Despite the massive loss of life and property together with their industrial capacity, the Japanese continued to fight. During the nine months from November 1944 more people

died in Japan than the total number of the Japanese armed forces killed throughout the war. Over 100sq miles of industrial heartland had been laid waste and still the war continued. It was not until 6 August 1945 when the first atom bomb - Little Boy - was dropped by B-29 *Enola Gay* on the city of Hiroshima. The dropping of this bomb resulted in the death of some 78,000 people - less than the 9 March attack on Tokyo. With no reaction from the Japanese Government a second bomb - Fat Boy - was dropped on 9 August by another B-29, named *Bock's Car* after its usual pilot, over the city of Nagasaki. This led to another 35,000 deaths but even then it took the Japanese five days to surrender. If an invasion of Japan had been required it was estimated that there would have been in the order of 1.5 million further lives lost.

B-29 production continued postwar and by 1946 3,970 had been delivered although orders for a further 5,092 were cancelled.

OPPOSITE: Close-up of *Fifi*'s nose showing its unusual streamlined cockpit.

ABOVE: Plane Sailing's Catalina is currently painted in a Royal Canadian Air Force colour scheme. The wingtip floats are seen here lowered for landing on water.

The Consolidated P3Y was designed in 1933. It first flew on 28 March 1935 and the initial 60 for the USN entered service in 1936. During 1935 a Catalina set a world distance record by flying from Panama to San Francisco - a distance of 3,300 miles. This demonstrated the long range which was to prove crucial during the later war years. It was also capable of carrying up to 2,000lb (907kg) of bombs, which is why the P3Y designation was changed to PBY.

At the time of Pearl Harbor, the PBY was the only long range aircraft available within the US military in quantity apart from the B-17 Flying Fortress. A US Navy PBY Catalina was the first to spot the Japanese fleet near Midway enabling the USN to intercept and destroy the numerically superior enemy force at the Battle of Midway.

The PBY was ordered for the RAF and RN as the Catalina. It was a No 210 Squadron aircraft that spotted the *Bismarck* making for a safe harbour in France. As a result the Royal

Navy launched an attack and successfully destroyed this dangerous German battleship. By the time the war ended, RAF Catalinas had been responsible for destroying or seriously damaging one in seven of the total U-boats hit by RAF Coastal Command.

The PBY soon became recognised for its versatility with search and rescue, reconnaissance and tactical bombing missions being undertaken as well as general transport and maritime patrol.

OPPOSITE TOP: The UK-based Catalina of Plane Sailing flying in the RAF markings of Flg Off J A Cruikshank from No 210 Squadron. He was awarded the Victoria Cross for pressing home an attack on a German U-boat despite having been wounded 79 times by the U-boat's anti-aircraft gunfire.

OPPOSITE BOTTOM: The Lockheed Ventura/Harpoon was based on the Lodestar and flown by the USAAF, RAF, and USN as a bomber, carrying 2,500lb of bombs, depth charges or torpedoes. This is the CAF's ex-USN PV-2 Harpoon.

ABOVE AND OPPOSITE: This CAF SB2C-5 Helldiver is the last flying example of the 7,200 aircraft built. It has been painted in the markings of the carrier USS *Franklin*, CV-13.

The design of the Curtiss SB2 Helldiver started in 1939. Due to a number of problems the flight of the first production aircraft was delayed until June 1942 and the first combat mission was flown in November 1943. Once in service, the SB2C was an extremely capable aircraft, delivering bombs or depth charges with pin-point accuracy. It also proved versatile in that it could be used to strafe with cannon, rockets and machine-gun fire. The majority of Helldivers built were delivered to the USMC although it was also operated by the US Navy and Royal Navy as well as the USAAF as the A-25A Shrike.

After the war a number of Helldivers saw service with foreign navies. Helldivers remained in US military service until June 1949 as the Navy's last pure dive bomber.

ABOVE: A TBM-3E Avenger of the CAF Rocky Mountain Wing. The Grumman Avenger was a carrier-based torpedo-carrying attack aircraft which first took to the air as the XBTF-1 Avenger on 1 August 1941. It was destined to become a major player in the naval battles in the Pacific Theatre. Early in 1942 an order was placed and within five months deliveries were under way. But the entry of the Avenger into combat at Midway was a disaster when five of the six aircraft launched were shot down and the Japanese target not hit. However, it soon lived up to its name and began playing havoc on enemy shipping.

The demand for the TBF stretched Grumman's capacity and, as a result, Grumman only built 2,293 TBF-1s and Eastern Aircraft, a division of General Motors, continued the production under licence. The Eastern-built Avengers were designated TBMs. Nearly 9,836 Avengers were built of which 958 served with the Royal Navy; these were initially named Tarpon but later renamed Avenger. The Royal New Zealand Air Force was another user. The Avenger remained in US Navy service until 1954.

OPPOSITE TOP: Tony Haig-Thomas lifts off in his TBM-3F Avenger for another display.

OPPOSITE BOTTOM: Being a carrier-based aircraft, the wings of the Avenger need to fold to save space in the cramped confines. Grumman's unique Sto-Wing enables the wing to fold back rather than vertically as demonstrated on the Cavanaugh TBM-3E.

BRITISH

ABOVE: The first Blenheim to be restored, V6028 coded GB-D of No 105 Squadron, was the result of 12 years' work of transformation from Bolingbroke RCAF 10038. Sadly, only one month after it had returned to the air, the only airworthy Blenheim was lost due to pilot error. Such was the strength of the restoration team, however, that with strong public support, within a short time they had selected another airframe and began the restoration process once again.

The Bristol Blenheim resulted from the owner of the *Daily Mail*, Lord Rothermere, requesting a design for the fastest twin-engined, six-seat, private transport aircraft. Bristol Aeroplane Co was already constructing a similar aircraft. It flew for the first time on 12 April 1935 and during test flying it reached 307mph (495km/h) which was faster than any current RAF fighter. Impressed with the performance, Lord Rothermere presented the aircraft to the Nation. The Air Ministry took immediate interest and investigated the possibility of the design becoming a bomber. Although not as straightforward as first envisaged, the prototype Blenheim took to the air on 25 June 1936.

When World War 2 broke out 1,089 Blenheims were in service while other bombers were only available in small numbers. The Blenheim was the first RAF aircraft to fly an operational mission as a recce flight over Germany and a number made the first bombing raid the following day. The Blenheim made a catalogue of other firsts from the first aircraft in the world to fly with air-to-air radar to the first RAF aircraft to sink a U-boat and later a Japanese submarine.

By 1940 the performance margin had been eroded in favour of Luftwaffe fighters but with few alternative aircraft the Blenheim continued to be used and was shot down in numbers that would have been unacceptable in any other circumstances.

OPPOSITE TOP: The second Blenheim to be restored was completed as Z5722 G-BPIV by the Aircraft Restoration Company and painted black as a night intruder with codes WM-Z of No 68 Squadron. When locating some vital components, they were offered the shorter nose of a Mark I which had been converted into an electric car.

OPPOSITE BOTTOM: The remains of the fuselage of Bolingbroke RCAF 10201 (a Canadian-built Blenheim) was the starting point for this restoration together with the wings from RCAF 9703. Using experience from the first Blenheim rebuild, John Romain and his team under the leadership of Graham Warner managed to complete this aircraft in just five years.

Top: With wings folded, the Firefly starts its engines before the crowd ready for another display. The Fairey Firefly carrier-based fighter-recce aircraft first flew on 22 December 1941 and was found to be extremely capable. Bomber and nightfighter were soon added to its roles. Such was the success of the initial design that the Firefly I remained in front line service until shortly after the end of the war. Most of the Firefly operations were confined to the Indian Ocean and Pacific Theatre. Production ceased in April 1956 with 1,702 aircraft built.

Above: The BBMF Lancaster with nose art reflecting 140 operational sorties - a Bomber Command record.

Opposite: The Royal Navy Historic Flight Fairey Firefly AS5 in the Korean War markings of No 812 Squadron flies in formation with a pair of Swordfish.

ABOVE: The BBMF Lancaster, PA474, painted with codes PM-M2 representing Nos 103 and 576 Squadrons with 140 mission nose art.

LEFT: Powered by the Rolls-Royce Merlin, visible on PA474 are the nose art markings of No IX Squadron coded WS-J *Jonnie Walker* whose crew was presented with a case of whisky after dropping a 12,000lb 'Tallboy' bomb on the *Tirpitz* .

OPPOSITE: The rear gun turret was equipped with either four .303in or .50in Browning machine-guns and would be a lonely location on lengthy operations. This turret on PA474 has been restored and is even fitted with dummy ammunition.

The Avro Lancaster is the RAF's most famous bomber. It was developed from the Manchester, first flew on 9 January 1941 and was the last British heavy bomber to enter operational service during World War 2.

First Lancaster deliveries were made to No 44 Squadron in late 1941. It was capable of carrying virtually any bombs. The most famous were the Barnes Wallis bouncing bombs which were dropped by No 617 (Dambuster) Squadron on the Mohne, Eder and Sorpe dams in the German Ruhr valley. A number were also modified to carry the 22,000lb (9,979kg) 'Grand Slam' which was the heaviest air-dropped bomb of the war.

The 7,377 Lancasters built delivered 63.8% of all bombs dropped by Bomber Command during the war, a total of 608,612 tons of bombs on 156,000 missions. The last operational RAF Lancaster was retired in February 1954.

ABOVE AND OPPOSITE: The de Havilland Mosquito T3 operated by British Aerospace and flown in the markings of No 633 Squadron with D-Day stripes.

The de Havilland DH98 Mosquito was a superb aircraft that nearly didn't happen due to the fact that a wooden aircraft was considered a backward step and metal aircraft were the vogue. Supported by Air Chief Marshal Sir Wilfred Freeman - the then Air Member of the Air Council for Development and Production, he ordered 50 of 'Freeman's Folly' while the aircraft was still on the drawing board. First flown on 25 November 1940, critics were then rapidly converted.

Construction of the Mosquito was primarily of balsa wood covered with birch laminations and Sitka spruce. The first operational sortie took-off on 18 September 1941 but this had to be abandoned en route due to technical problems. However, success was to follow quickly and the Mosquito was to prove a top performer. Some of the later variants were developed to increase their bomb load to be capable of carrying a 4,000lb bomb to Berlin - just half of the bomb load of a B-24 with one fifth of the crew and no fighter cover needed!

ABOVE: Fairey Swordfish II W5856 of the Royal Navy Historic Flight painted in the markings of No 810 Squadron as for the summer exercises of 1939.

Initially referred to as the Fairey TSR (Torpedo Spotter Reconnaissance) biplane, it was designed to meet the Naval spec S.15/33. Powered by a 690hp Bristol Pegasus engine and with folding wings, the TSR could carry a single 18in torpedo under its fuselage.

The Swordfish, or 'Stringbag' as it was affectionately named, entered service in 1936. By the time war broke the FAA was equipped with 13 Swordfish-equipped front line squadrons. Although obsolete in design compared to most other aircraft at the time, the Swordfish was to soldier on until the end of the war in Europe.

The capabilities of the Swordfish were clearly illustrated during operations around Norway in 1940 and the attack on Taranto harbour in November 1940. This was when 20 Swordfish managed to cripple the Italian Naval Fleet while it lay in the 'safety' of Taranto harbour. As a result the Italian Navy was to cause the Allies little further trouble.

OPPOSITE: Short Sunderland ML814 is now part of the Kermit Weeks Fantasy of Flight based at Polk City, Florida and operates from Lake Agnes. She is currently lacking the nose gun turret which was removed when she was civilianised in 1963. It is to be hoped that one will be located soon and then ML814 can be restored back to her former self.

The Short Sunderland was designed for the maritime patrol role using experience gained from Shorts' involvement with the 'Empire' class flying boats. The first Sunderland entered service in June 1938 and by the outbreak of World War 2 a total of 27 had been delivered. Besides operating as a maritime patrol aircraft and on anti-submarine patrols (with 58 U-boats sunk or severely damaged), the Sunderland was used for carrying passengers and freight and as an air ambulance.

By the end of the war 20 squadrons of the RAF, RAAF and RCAF were operating the Sunderland. Production ended in June 1946 by which time 749 aircraft had been built. The last RAF flight of a Sunderland was on 20 May 1959, which was also the last flight by a flying boat in RAF service.

GERMAN

ABOVE: There are no genuine Heinkel He111s flying although there are several static. The Spanish AF ordered a number of CASA-built versions - the 2111 - and these remained in service until the late 1960s. Despite their being powered by the Rolls-Royce Merlin a number of these aircraft were 'borrowed' for the making of the film *The Battle of Britain*. This particular CASA 2111E operated by the Arizona Wing of the Confederate AF was once the personal plane of General Franco and is now painted to represent a He111.

The Heinkel He111 light bomber dates back to 1933 when design began. It was first flown on 24 February 1935 despite an arms ban in Germany. This was achieved by cunningly disguising the aircraft as a civilian 10-passenger airline transport aircraft.

The He111 was blooded during the Spanish Civil War and saw considerable success but mainly against unarmed or poorly defended targets. During the Blitzkrieg on Poland the Luftwaffe offensive relied on light bomber types but the odds were not so much in the He111s' favour and 78 were lost.

When they were used against the British the loss rate was in the region of 25per cent and the Luftwaffe had to change tactics using the He111 primarily as a night bomber. However, despite its drawbacks, the He111 was a popular aircraft with its pilots and production continued until 1944. A total of around 7,500 was built including postwar production in Romania and Spain where CASA continued to construct 263 examples powered by Rolls-Royce Merlins as late as 1956.

OPPOSITE TOP: The cockpit of the CAF CASA 2111 is now fitted with modern radios and provides good forward visibility.

OPPOSITE BOTTOM: The bomb racks require the bombs to be loaded vertically through the bomb bay; they are then stored either side of the fuselage.

JAPANESE

ABOVE AND OPPOSITE BOTTOM: No examples of the Nakajima B5N 'Kate' survived the war. Those that appear at the CAF airshows were modified from two T-6 airframes for the film *Tora Tora Tora*. They provided realistic replicas and help the CAF to perform dramatic set pieces for the airshow crowds.

The Nakajima B5N was powered by a 770hp Hikari engine. It first flew in 1937 and entered production as a 1,000hp Nakajima Sakae 11-powered light bomber or torpedo bomber. A number were subsequently used during the attacks on China. Many were converted to B5N1-K trainers when production switched to B5N2. Some 40 B5N1 'Kates' from the carrier *Soryu* were included in the force that attacked Pearl Harbor. While the 'Kate' continued to be used in the anti-submarine role throughout the war, it was vulnerable to any fighter attack.

OPPOSITE TOP: The Allied instruction that the entire Japanese war machine had to be destroyed has resulted in the elimination of virtually all Japanese World War 2 aircraft. The majority of the survivors are those captured by the Allies and taken home for testing. No original airworthy 'Vals' exist. This particular aircraft is based on a Vultee BT-13 Valiant with various modifications to represent the Aichi D3A; it was built for the film *Tora Tora Tora*.

The design of the Aichi D3A, code-named 'Val' by the Allies, commenced in 1936 and it entered production in 1937. The first Japanese all-metal low-winged monoplane dive bomber, it was the 'Val' that formed the largest part of the Japanese force which attacked Pearl Harbor. It was an effective aircraft especially in the hands of a skilled pilot as was clearly demonstrated in the Pacific campaign. When production of the D3A1 ended in 1942 a total of 478 aircraft had been built. These were followed by the more powerful D3A2 of which 816 were built.

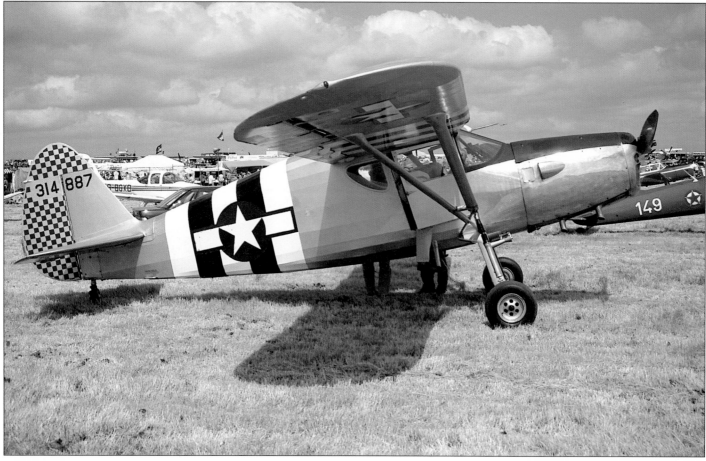

COMMUNICATIONS
AMERICAN

ABOVE: A Stinson AT-19 Reliant painted in Royal Navy colours. The AT-19 was based on the civilian Reliant, production of which stopped when the US entered the war. The few aircraft which were serving with the USAAC, USN and USCG had either been bought or impressed. The Royal Navy was the largest operator and production was reopened for a batch of 500 aircraft.

OPPOSITE TOP: Fairchild UC-21K Forwarder ordered for the USAAC as 44-83184 and actually delivered to the RAF as Argus III KK527; it sports a representative USAAC scheme.

OPPOSITE BOTTOM: Similarly, Fairchild UC-61A Forwarder ordered for the USAAC as 43-14887 was delivered to the RAF as HB614. The Fairchild UC-61 Forwarder (or Argus in British service) was developed from the Kreider-Reisner Model 24C three-seat touring aircraft of 1933. Almost 1,000 radial or in-line powered UC-61 Forwarders were ordered by the USAAC and some 830 were transferred to the RAF under Lend Lease arrangements as various marks of Argus mainly for the Air Transport Auxiliary.

TOP AND ABOVE: Originally designated O-49 when designed by Stinson as an AOP (Air Observation Post) for the USAAC, in 1942 the 334 O-49s were redesignated L-1 (L for liaison) with the L-1C model for the air ambulance role, the L-1D as a pilot trainer in glider pickup techniques and the L-1E and F models air ambulances fitted with floats. In summer 1940 Vultee took over Stinson (Vultee itself was taken over by Consolidated in 1943). 105 L-1s were received by the RAF as the Vigilant I.

OPPOSITE: The Aeronca L-3 Grasshopper (Top), Stinson L-5 Sentinel and Piper L-4 Grasshopper (Bottom) family of similar but smaller aircraft served during the war in large numbers as liaison and observation aircraft.

TOP: The Beech UC-43 Traveler was based on the civil D-17S. It was ordered by the USAAF and USN under a variety of designations for use in the utility role. In addition about 100 were supplied to the Royal Navy. This particular aircraft is painted in the markings of one presented to Prince Bernhardt of the Netherlands.

ABOVE: Large numbers of aircraft received nose art during the war: even the smaller were suitably adorned.

OPPOSITE: The OY-1 is the US Marine Corps version of the USAAC/USAAF L-5 Sentinel, 306 of which were purchased for use in support of its operations in the Pacific Theatre.

BRITISH

ABOVE: This Auster formation is led by Mk I LB375. Also in the formation are some postwar variants in the form of Auster AOP Mk VI TW536, Auster T7 WE569 and Auster AOP9 WZ662.

OPPOSITE TOP: The de Havilland Hornet Moth originally flew in 1934 and 168 had been built when production ceased in 1938. When it became obvious that war was imminent, large numbers of suitable civilian aircraft were impressed into the military for a wide range of roles. W9385 was typical of this arrangement. This particular Hornet Moth served during World War 2 with RAF Coastal Command's No 3 Coastal Patrol Flight and later was used by several ground training units. She survived the war to be returned back to civilian ownership.

OPPOSITE BOTTOM: The Auster originates from a design by the American Taylorcraft company. - the Taylorcraft D and tandem Model B - which was built under licence in the UK by Taylorcraft Ltd. Used extensively by the British Forces in the AOP role named the Auster I, this aircraft initially saw service with No 651 Squadron, RAF. Due to their role, the AOP squadrons were strange in that their aircraft were mainly manned by Army personnel attached to the RAF. The AOP role required the Auster to circle a battlefield and report back to the army artillery units corrections for their gunfire. This then ensured greater effectiveness of the artillery but made the Auster a prime target for the enemy. In addition to the AOP role the Auster was widely used for communications and as an air ambulance because of its ability to get in and out of small isolated locations. 100 examples of the Mk I were built but found to be under-powered and were rapidly augmented by the main variants in the form of the Mk III with 470 built, 254 Mk IVs and 804 Mk Vs. The Auster was flown by a total of 16 RAF squadrons in Burma, Europe and the Middle East.

TOP AND OPPOSITE: The Westland Lysander prototype first flew in 1936 as an Army co-operation aircraft and entered RAF service in June 1938. It suffered from being very vulnerable to enemy aircraft, but in 1941 was given a new lease of life ferrying Allied agents and supplies into German-occupied Europe. The Lysander excelled at this sort of operation and provided a vital service.

ABOVE: The Slingsby Type 6 Kirby Kite first flew in 1935. Only 25 were built and most were impressed into military service in 1940 as the first military glider. They were initially used by the newly formed Glider Training Squadron to train the first Army glider pilots. Later larger gliders become a vital means of transporting troops onto the battlefield and saw extensive use during World War 2 - especially during the D-Day landings and the battle of Arnhem.

ABOVE: The Fieseler Fi156 Storch was designed for the army co-operation, casualty evacuation and communications role and first flew in 1936. It was fitted with leading edge slots and full-span flaps which gave the Fi156 an extremely slow speed to the extent that in a 25mph (40km/h) wind it would virtually hover. Because of these STOL capabilities, the Fi156 was able to get into and out of very small unprepared strips and became extremely popular. A total of 2,549 was built during the war with production also being carried out in the Fieseler-controlled Morane-Saulnier factory in France. As can be seen the name Storch (stork) was apposite to the spindly Fi156. This is a postwar aircraft built as a Morane MS505 and operated by the Aircraft Restoration Co at Duxford.

LEFT AND OPPOSITE: The Messerschmitt Bf108 Taifun (Typhoon) was designed in 1933 and flew the following year. As with the Bf109, the Bf designation may seem odd - it's because both types were designed by Willy Messerschmitt while he was employed by Bayerische Flugzeugwerke AG before he became Managing Director and the company became Messerschmitt AG in 1938.

During World War 2 the Bf108 served with the Luftwaffe ferrying pilots, personnel and urgent supplies and even target towing. Production later transferred to the SNCA factory in France and a total of 885 was completed by the end of the war.

This Nord 1002 Pingouin version of the Bf108 is one of the 285 which were built postwar. Owned and operated by farmer Lindsey Walton, when painted in Luftwaffe markings she became one of the first 'enemy' aircraft to fly at UK air displays in 1973 and continues to be popular today.

GERMAN

TRANSPORT
AMERICAN

ABOVE AND OPPOSITE TOP: The Douglas C-47 Skytrain is better known by its RAF name - Dakota. This DC-3 derivative and the Curtiss C-46 Commando (Above) provided the Allies with the bulk of their transport fleet during the war. The C-47 was built in larger numbers - nearly 11,000 including the USN R4D version compared to just over 3,000 C-46s.

OPPOSITE BOTTOM AND TOP: The Beech C-45 Expediter fulfilled the smaller communications, transport, training and utility roles. It was used extensively by the USAAF as the UC-45, the USN as the JRB and the RN and RAF (Expediter I and II).

ABOVE AND LEFT: As with most US World War 2 transports, the Lockheed Lodestar was developed from an existing civil airliner, in this case the Model 18. Initially a number of C-56 and C-57 variants were ordered or impressed prior to subsequent orders for 361 C-60s. In addition a number went to the RAF primarily in the Near and Middle East. *Lady Lodestar* is C-60A 42-55884 operated by the Confederate Air Force.

OPPOSITE TOP: The Douglas C-41 was the first military version of the DC-3 airliner and was delivered for the USAAC's Chief-of-Staff General 'Hap' Arnold. The only example built, this C-41 has been restored back to the original USAAC VIP markings by her American owner, Otis Spunkmeyer.

OPPOSITE BOTTOM: The Douglas C-47 was originally ordered in 1940 and was to become the most successful military transport ever. Versatility could have been its middle name as the C-47 could carry a wide range of loads including cargo, troops and stretchers. It could drop paratroops and tow gliders, even snatching up gliders from the ground while in flight.

ABOVE: The Junkers Ju52 was originally flown as a single-engined transport in 1930 but developed into the Ju52/3m with three licence-built Pratt & Whitney Hornet engines in 1932. Production soon followed with BMW engines and eventually 230 were delivered to Lufthansa. Deliveries to airlines worldwide of this corrugated duralumin-skinned aircraft were extensive and even included a version fitted with floats.

In 1934 the first of a military variant, the Ju52/3mg3e, was developed in secret for the Luftwaffe as a heavy bomber and fitted with machine-guns. During 1934-5 some 450 Ju52/3ms were delivered to the Luftwaffe. In 1936 the Ju52/3m was the first German aircraft to be flown in the Spanish Civil War with the Condor Legion. Initially they were used to transport 10,000 Moorish troops to Spain and then used as bombers against Republican targets until replaced by the Dornier Do18. At the end of this war 25 Ju52s were retained as transports for the Spanish Air Force.

During the early days of World War 2 the Ju52 was an integral part of the German war machine's Blitzkrieg through Europe. Paratroops would be dropped forward enabling swift victories across Europe before any proper defensive strategies could be put in place. 547 Ju52s were reputed to have been used against Poland in 1939 and in 1940 475 were used together with 45 DFS230 gliders against the Netherlands, but here they sustained 167 losses. In Norway alone, nearly 600

Ju52s flew a total of 3,018 sorties during which over 29,000 men, 2,300 tons of supplies and 300,000gal of fuel were delivered.

As the war progressed the slow, lumbering Ju52 fell foul of faster, heavily armed fighters and anti-aircraft fire. In support of the Afrika Korps in 1943 the Ju52s were required to fly resupply missions due to Allied blockades of ports in the Mediterranean. On 18 April 1943 52 of a force of 100 Ju52s were shot down. During the period 5-22 April, 432 German transports were shot down of which most would have been Ju52s. This was for the loss of only 35 Allied aircraft.

A total of 3,845 Ju52 was thought to have been built and quite a number were flown in military and civilian hands after the end of the war. In addition postwar production in France as the AAC1 and Spain as the C-352 ensured that numbers of the Ju52 family remain.

This is an ex-Spanish AF CASA C-352 which remained operational with this air force until the 1970s.

OPPOSITE: Ju52/3m D-AQUI (actually D-CDLH) of the Lufthansa Heritage Flight is the subject of a beat-up by a Mosquito during a display at Duxford. Part of Lufthansa's fleet of airliners, this Ju52/3m remains a fully serviceable airliner and tours around Europe.

German

TRAINERS
AMERICAN

ABOVE: In 1934 the Stearman company became a subsidiary of Boeing after producing the prototype Model X70 primary trainer which won the USAAC basic trainer competition. The Stearman 75 became the Boeing Kaydet with US Army designations PT-13/17/18 and 27. The USN designated the Kaydet the NS-1: later models were designated N2S. The first orders for 61 NS-1s were placed by the US Navy followed later by 26 PT-13s for the USAAC. By 1939 orders were gushing in for additional Kaydets and by the time production ceased in 1945 over 10,000 had been built.

This ex-US Navy N2S-3 is one of numerous Kaydet survivors - the aircraft was supplied to many countries outside the USA including Peru, Venezuela, Great Britain and China.

OPPOSITE TOP: The Vultee Valiant family resulted from a USAAC proposal for a multi-purpose trainer and fighter. An initial order was placed for 300 of a simplified basic trainer variant designated BT-13. This was then the largest USAAC order for a trainer. A similar requirement for the US Navy resulted in the SNV. Eventually, when production ceased in summer 1944 11,537 Valiants had been built including the more powerful BT-15. The Valiant was the standard USAAF basic trainer until superseded in 1943 by the North American AT-6 Texan.

OPPOSITE BOTTOM: The Fairchild PT-19 basic trainer was the military version of the M-62. Sales commenced in 1940 but Fairchild was soon so swamped with the orders that licenced production lines were opened. Airframe production then outstripped engines and the 220hp Continental R-670 was substituted for the Ranger L-440 in 1942, resulting in the PT-23. The PT-23 and PT-26, which was given the name Cornell by the RCAF, were adopted as the standard primary trainer for the Commonwealth Air Training Scheme and built by Fleet Aircraft Ltd, Toronto. The more advanced PT-26 was fitted with an enclosed heated cockpit for the colder Canadian environment plus duplicated blind flying and navigation instruments.

This PT-23 is one of the few survivors of over 13,000 of the PT-19/23/26 family that were built by US and Canadian factories.

TOP: The North American AT-6 Texan was first produced in 1939, developed as an advanced training aircraft from the 1935 NA-16. Orders followed for the USAAC and the US Navy in whose hands it was designated SNJ. Further orders were placed by the RAF, with whom it served as the Harvard. Over 15,000 had been built when production ended.

ABOVE: The Ryan PT-16 was the military designation for the civilian S-T-A basic trainer. In 1940 30 PT-20s were ordered

followed by 100 PT- 21s for the USAAC and 100 NR-1s for the US Navy with the 132hp Kinner R-440 engine. A further order followed for 1,023 PT-22 Recruits with the 160hp Kinner R-540 engine. Large numbers of Ryan trainers were produced including aircraft supplied to Guatemala, China, Honduras, Mexico.

OPPOSITE: The USN followed the USAAC's lead and ordered 100 of the Ryan PT-22 trainer, designating it NR-1.

BRITISH

OPPOSITE TOP: The Miles M14 Magister entered service with the RAF in 1937 as its first monoplane basic trainer at a time when the biplane was still dominant. The Magister saw service throughout the war and many of the more than 1,200 built passed to civil flying afterwards. Magister Mk I P6382/G-AJDR is one of the few airworthy Magisters left today. It is flown by the Shuttleworth Collection.

OPPOSITE BOTTOM: The de Havilland DH82b Queen Bee was developed as a remote-controlled naval target aircraft. Based on the DH82a Tiger Moth the Queen Bee differed in that its fuselage was of all wood construction rather than the Tiger Moth's canvas and metal frame. LF858/G-BLUZ was one of 412 Queen Bees built between 1933 and 1941. Privately owned, it is thought to be one of only two remaining airworthy.

ABOVE: The de Havilland Tiger Moth was designed as a training aircraft and first flew in October 1931. It was to become the RAF's most famous ab initio trainer and by September 1939 over 1,000 were in service. It was operated by the RAF from 1932 until 1947 by the Elementary and Reserve Flying Schools and gave flying training to almost all wartime RAF aircrew. In the region of 8,800 Tiger Moths were built all told, including some 420 Queen Bees. Over 3,000 of these were built overseas in Australia, Canada and New Zealand for the Commonwealth Air Training Plan, with many going to South Africa, India and Rhodesia. This privately owned Tiger Moth, DF128, has been restored back to RAF No 6 Reserve Flying School colours.

RUSSIAN

ABOVE: The Yak-11 was designed as an intermediate and advanced trainer and first flew in 1946. Powered by a Shvetsov ASh-21, the Yak-11 retains much ancestry of the later World War 2 Yakovlev family of fighters. It has a similar wing shape and metal construction together with the metal and fabric fuselage. With fuel injection, the Yak-11 is also a very capable aerobatic two-seat aircraft but could be fitted with a machine-gun or even carry practice bombs or rockets on pylons.

Code-named 'Moose' by NATO the aircraft saw extensive service with the Soviet and Warsaw Pact air forces. Over 3,800 examples were built in Russia with a further 700 built by LET of Czechoslovakia. During the 1970s, the Yak-11 was virtually unheard of in the west apart from one example which made

a forced landing on Cyprus, was impounded and later restored in the UK. In the early 1980s the Egyptian Air Force decided to dispose of its inventory of Yak-11s together with six containers of spares. Sold as a single batch, 41 Yak-11s plus four Yak-18s were purchased by a group of warbird enthusiasts. Today many of these aircraft have been or are currently being fully restored to flying condition.

This photograph shows Yak-11 G-KYAK, which was EAF590 of the Egyptian Air Force until the pilot defected to Israel in 1964. In 1978 she was acquired by Robs Lamplough, transported to the UK for restoration at Duxford and took to the air again in 1981. She has since been sold to Flying Legends in France as F-AZHQ.

SWISS

TOP AND ABOVE: The Pilatus P2 was designed as an advanced trainer and first flew in 1945. The first 27 were built as pilot trainers while the balance of 26 were built for weapons and observer training. Powered by a 465hp Argus As410 engine, they were capable of operating from the high altitude airfields of the Alps. They were built using many parts from Swiss stocks of Bf109 components.

INDEX